LET'S GET READY FOR WORK

Work Readiness Solutions Guide & Workbook – "Preparing for the Workforce"

Norman L. Collins, Sr., PhD

OuttaDNorm Solutions, LLC

Copyright © 2025 by Norman L. Collins, Sr., PhD

All rights reserved. No part of this publication may be reproduced, distributed, or transmitted in any form or by any means without prior written permission.

Norman L. Collins, Sr., PhD
OuttaDNorm Solutions, LLC

Book Formatting and Distribution Services
Rain Publishing
www.RainPublishing.com

LET'S GET READY FOR WORK/ Norman L. Collins, Sr., PhD. -- 1st ed.
ISBN 979-8-9927864-6-0

FOREWORD

A number of people who are in search of employment experience find that despite their education, experience, and skills, they are still faced with significant barriers to employment as a result of not having obtained appropriate and/or sufficient work readiness skills, which is preventing them from obtaining sustainable employment opportunities in a career that they would otherwise be qualified for.

Soft skills, or employability skills, have become the hard skills of today's workforce. Research conducted by Harvard University, the Carnegie Foundation, and Stanford Research Center concluded that 85% of job success comes from having well-developed soft skills, and only 15% of job success comes from technical skills and knowledge. Yet, employers say that applicants are unprepared for work because of their lack of these soft, employability skills, or termed work readiness skills.

H4U2 Consulting LLC has developed and produced this Workforce Solutions Guide that has been used to facilitate workshops and seminars to assist those in the job/career search market, which includes information and interactive tools and activities that are designed to prepare individuals to engage in a successful job search as well as securing and maintaining sustainable employment.
So ……

"Let's Get Ready for Work!"

Dedication

This guide is dedicated to all of my mentors who have provided me with the opportunity of employment, including the late Dr. McKinley Martin, Sr., Ms. Verna Gray, Dr. Steve Ellis, Christopher Rivera, LaToya Brower, Michael Taylor, JB Buxton, as well as those who have supported and encouraged me through my periods of unemployment including my family and close friends. Moreover, I am eternally grateful for the grace and mercy God has provided me on my journey and the fortitude to keep moving during difficult times.

TABLE OF CONTENTS

WHAT DO I KNOW ABOUT ME?	1
BARRIERS TO EMPLOYMENT	3-7
BE B.A.D.	9-16
RESUME WRITING	17-23
COVER LETTER/THANK YOU LETTER	25-31
INTERVIEW SKILLS	33-51
NETWORKING & COMMUNICATION	53-67
WORK ETHICS & ETIQUETTE	69-79
WORK READINESS PRE-TEST / POST-TEST	81-84

WHAT DO I KNOW ABOUT ME?

Self-awareness is the first step in creating what you want and mastering your life. Where you focus your attention, your emotions, reactions, personality, and behavior determine where you go in life. Having self-awareness allows you to see where your thoughts and emotions are taking you. It also allows you to take control of your emotions, behavior, and personality so you can make changes you want. Until you are aware of your thoughts, emotions, words, and behavior, you will have difficulty making changes in the direction of your life.

The following questions are designed to increase your self-awareness and self-actualization. In other words, the more you know about yourself, the more you can convey to employers in an effort to promote your readiness to work. Be sure to answer each question as honestly as you know it to be.

What do I think about the most? Why?

What makes me happy, sad, or angry?

What motivates me?

What stresses me out?

What do I like to do?

What do I not like to do?

How do I view myself?

What skills do I have?

What am I passionate about?

What are my achievements?

Do I need to change anything about me?

What skills do I have?

What am I passionate about?

What are my achievements?

Do I need to change anything about me?

BARRIERS TO EMPLOYMENT

A physical condition or personal situation can make it hard to find or keep a job.

Many job seekers experience one or more barriers to employment during their careers. Although this makes finding or keeping a job more difficult, it's not impossible. Some barriers, such as a lack of transportation, are temporary and easier to address than others.

Common Barriers to Employment

- Age
- Disabilities
- Criminal record
- Disadvantaged background
- Domestic violence
- Drug and/or alcohol abuse
- Lack of education
- Employer biases
- Has a child
- Housing issues or homelessness
- Ineffective job search skills
- Lacks basic and soft skills
- Limited English/French proficiency
- Long-term welfare recipient
- Mental illness
- Needs training
- Needs childcare assistance
- No transportation
- Gaps in employment
- Lack of self-confidence/low self-esteem
- Wanting to give up/burnout
- Not understanding modern recruitment practices
- Inability to identify transferable skills
- Lack of formal qualifications
- Lack of IT skills
- Physical health issues
- Little or no work history
- Sick family member
- Learning disabilities
- Children's Services involvement
- Suspended driver's license
- Legal problems
- Social isolation
- Financial issues/Debt
- Illiteracy
- Appearance
- Lack of personal hygiene

Addressing Barriers in the Job Hunt

In order to be successful in your job hunt, you need to be the type of employee that employers want to hire. This is true for every job seeker, not just those with barriers. Employers want people with the right skills to do the work, a personality that fits the company culture, and a good work ethic.

All job seekers need to focus on their qualifications and positive traits, not on their barriers. If an employer asks about your barrier in a job interview, be prepared to talk about how it will not affect your ability to be a good employee:

- **Identify the barrier.** Sometimes the employer doesn't understand what the barrier is or how it does and does not affect your ability to work.
- **Get some perspective on the barrier.** Only talk about how the barrier might affect your ability to do your job or interact with people. If the barrier does not affect your job, then make sure the employer knows this.
- **Come up with workable solutions and goals.** Be proactive and give the employer suggestions as to how you can minimize your barrier or find ways for it not to affect your job. Talk with an employment advisor to get suggestions.

> What are some barriers you have encountered in your employment search?
>
> How might you overcome these barriers?

Don't be afraid, ashamed, or embarrassed to seek or ask for help. There are ways to overcome these barriers:
- Have a positive attitude about getting help and finding work.
- Seek out counseling, transitional, and assistance services, if you need them, to find employment. Start with this list of employment training programs.
- Participate in drug, alcohol, and mental health rehab services, if necessary.
- Find affordable training and ways to help pay for training.
- Use community services for help with basic needs and English as a second language tutoring.
- Learn how your disability can be accommodated at work.
- Look into available support services, like childcare and transportation.
- Seek out resources to help you if you are an ex-offender or have a poor work history.

How to Find Resources to Help

If you can't overcome your barriers on your own, work with an employment advisor to learn about the resources and support available to you. An employment advisor can also provide a well-coordinated, overall support system to help you find training, counseling, basic needs assistance, help to find a job, and with continued support in the workplace and at home. Job counselors, WorkForce Centers, and case workers can serve as coaches and help you find out if you can get help for your particular situation. If you are struggling with more than one barrier, you may need to connect with different resources to help with each barrier.

Utilize Intermediaries

Intermediaries are organizations that focus on providing skill-enhancing opportunities or connections to potential employers. Their functions can include:
- Providing learning opportunities
- Providing support and community
- Connections you to potential employers

These types of organizations can include:
- Community-based non-profits
- Faith-based organizations
- Government-funded American Job Centers
- Staffing agencies
- Training organizations

What are the names of some intermediaries and resources can you identify in your area and/or community?

What type of services do they offer?

AVOIDING THE EMPLOYMENT GAP

Researchers suggest that the longer you are out of work, the harder it is to find it. Consider short and long-term strategies and think of your own ways to redefine what work looks like for you. Engage in short-term actions.

- Investigate part-time work
    - Provides income to you and your family
    - Reduces the gap on your resume
    - Keeps you active and interacting with others in a professional setting
    - Has the potential to develop into full-time employment
    - Keeps your skills sharp and/or helps you develop new skills

- Explore staffing agencies
    - Potential for permanent positions
    - Opportunity to hone your skills
    - More empathetic regarding employment gaps

- Consider volunteering
    - Reduces the gap on your resume
    - Keeps your skills sharp and provides opportunities to gain new skills
    - Assists in maintaining a routine
    - Creates new networks
    - Feeds your interests
    - Fosters a deeper sense of appreciation
    - Stimulates positivity

- Give serious thought to creating or starting your own business
    - Opportunity to do what you are passionate about
    - Builds upon your critical thinking and research skills
    - Invokes the need for networking
    - Fills the boredom gap
    - Provides for potential, ongoing income
    - Allows you to be your own boss

Have you considered part-time employment? If not, why?

List some staffing agencies with whom you might find employment.

Do you volunteer anywhere? List some organizations where you can volunteer to use the skills you currently have.

Have you considered starting your own business? If not, what would that business be?

BE B.A.D.

Building self-confidence, Adjust your attitude, Doing your Dreams

BUILDING SELF-CONFIDENCE

Self-confidence is a good feeling about yourself and your capabilities. So, if you're a self-confident person, it simply means that you feel good about who you are, and you also feel good about your ability to achieve things you want to achieve.

Digging a little deeper, you can think of self-confidence as being a good feeling about yourself and your capabilities that:

- Comes from the way you think about yourself and your capabilities

- Naturally makes you happier and more successful in life

- Can remain in any situation or circumstance, even without support from others or without material possessions

Self-confidence is something that benefits you in a powerful way, because not only is it a good feeling that naturally makes you happier and more successful, but it's also something that you can develop and maintain in any situation or circumstance.
This is because it is self-confidence that comes from within you, not confidence that comes from other people or things that are external to you.

The following are ways in which your self-esteem is exhibited to others:

- **Act the part.**
  Your body language can instantly demonstrate self-assuredness, or it can scream insecurity. Present yourself in a way that says you are ready to master or take command of any situation. If you look confident and act the part you aspire to reach, you'll not only feel in control, people will have much more confidence in you as well.

  Hold your head high, sit up straight, gently bring your shoulders back to align your spine, and look directly at the other person when interacting. Avoid a limp handshake and maintain good eye contact while someone is speaking to you.

- **Dress the part.**
  When you look better, you feel better. If you choose clothing and accessories that fit you well, suit your industry and lifestyle, and make you feel good, this will automatically increase your self-esteem. Look like the part you want to play, or in other words, suit up for success. Don't be afraid to let your personality shine in your accessories. Bold jewelry or a colorful tie can be a focal point and a good conversation starter.

- **Speak assertively.**
  The next time you listen to your favorite speaker, be mindful of the way he or she delivers a speech. A great speaker speaks confidently, in a steady, rhythmic tone. Instead of the "ums" and "ahs" that interrupt flow, they use pauses to emphasize ideas.

  Adopt an assertive, but not aggressive, way of speaking that indicates your self-confidence. You will feel your self-esteem begin to rise. To be taken seriously, avoid high-pitched, nervous chatter or twittering giggles in your speech. People will listen to you more attentively when they see the leader radiate from within you.

- **Think and act positively.**
  Positive energy leads to positive outcomes, so set your mind to the can-do side of any situation, avoiding the negative self-talk that can make you feel less confident. Smile, laugh, and surround yourself with happy, positive people. You'll feel better, and the people with whom you work will enjoy your company.

  Keep a gratitude journal to remind yourself of the high points of your day and your accomplishments. You will develop more peace and confidence when you are in a grateful state of mind.

- **Take action.**
  There's more to being confident than just how you look. You must act the part. Walk up to a stranger at a networking event or accept a project you'd normally reject. Practice being self-confident, and soon it will become second nature.

  Inaction breeds doubt and fear, while action breeds confidence and courage. As an exercise, jot down your strengths and weaknesses. Most people will tell you to work on your weaknesses, but use what you've got and capitalize on your strengths instead. Once you put more energy into your positive traits, your confidence will start to shine through.

- **Be prepared.**
  Remember the five P's: Prior planning prevents poor performance. The more prepared you are, the more confident you'll feel about your expertise and competence. Preparation will help you avoid getting tripped up by life's unexpected glitches.

  Learn everything you can about your industry, your subject matter, your goals, and what drives you towards success. Before you start a task, first imagine how you want to feel once you've completed it. Don't try to accomplish too much at once. Break complex tasks up into small, bite-sized, manageable pieces.

  As U.S. Army General Creighton Williams Abrams Jr. once said, "When eating an elephant, take one bite at a time." If you have patience and perseverance, you are only steps away from a more confident you.

ADJUSTING YOUR ATTITUDE

An attitude is a settled way of thinking or feeling about someone or something, typically one that is reflected in a person's behavior. Attitudes have a direct effect on people, how things are handled, and outcomes.

NEGATIVE EFFECTS
- Undermines relations with others
- Missed opportunities for advancement
- Risk of loss of job security
- Low performance level
- Physical stress
- Creates an unwanted reputation
- Depressed and despaired outlook

POSITIVE EFFECTS
- Good relationships with family, peers, others
- Greater potential for advancement
- Better job security
- More cooperative and productive
- Less or no stress
- Favorable reputation
- Empowerment and control of your life

WAYS TO MAINTAIN A POSITIVE ATTITUDE

1. **Have a Morning Routine.** How you start your morning sets the tone for the rest of the day. Make sure that you have an attitude-boosting morning routine that puts you in a good mood so that you can start the day off right.

2. **Carry An Attitude of Happiness With You.** Instead of waiting for external things to make you happy, be happy, and then watch how that influences the things that go on around you. That is, instead of telling yourself that first something good has to happen, and then you'll be happy, be happy first. Happiness is an attitude, not a situation.

3. **Relish Small Pleasures.** Big pleasures—graduation, getting married, being promoted, having your book published—come too infrequently. Life is made up of tiny victories and simple pleasures. With the right mental attitude, watching the sunset, eating an ice cream cone, and walking barefoot on the grass are all you need to be filled with joy.

4. **Smile.** Smiling will give you an instantaneous attitude boost. Try smiling for a minute while you think of a happy memory or the last thing that made you smile. Smiling releases endorphins and serotonin, also known as the feel-good hormones. It's a lot easier to adopt a positive attitude when the chemicals being released by your body are conducive to well-being.

5. **Upload Positivity to Your Brain**. Read books with a positive message, listen to music with uplifting lyrics, and watch movies in which the protagonist's optimism helps him/her to overcome obstacles and win, despite the odds. Change your attitude for the better by uploading as much positivity into your brain as you possibly can.

6. **Take Responsibility**. At any moment, your attitude can be that of a victim or of a creator. The first step you need to take to shift from victim-mode to creator-mode is to take responsibility. Here's the attitude of a creator:
   - I create my life.
   - I am responsible for myself.
   - I'm in charge of my destiny.

7. **Have a Zen Attitude**. Think of life not as something that's happening to you, but as something that's happening for you. Look at any challenging situation, person, or event as a teacher that's been brought into your life to teach you something.

   The next time you find yourself thinking, "Why is this happening to me?" choose to have a Zen attitude instead. Ask yourself, "What am I supposed to learn or gain from this"? or "How will this help me grow and become a better, more enlightened being?"

8. **Be Proactive.** A reactive person allows others and external events to determine how they will feel. A proactive person decides how they will feel regardless of what may be going on around them. Be proactive by choosing your attitude and maintaining it throughout the day, regardless of what the day may bring.

9. **Change Your Thoughts**. Positive thoughts lead to a positive attitude, while negative thoughts lead to a negative attitude. Changing your attitude is as easy as hitting the "pause" button on what you're thinking and choosing to think different thoughts.

10. **Have a Purpose.** Having a purpose in life gives you a fixed point on the horizon to focus on, so that you can remain steady amid life's vicissitudes and challenges. Bringing meaning and purpose into your life—knowing why you are here—will do wonders for your attitude.

11. **Focus On the Good.** In order to have a positive attitude, focus on the good. Focus on the good in yourself, the good in your life, and the good in others.

12. **Stop Expecting Life to Be Easy.** The truth is, life gets tough at times for all of us. It can even be painful. But you're brave and resourceful, and you can take it. Know that sometimes things won't be easy, and adopt the attitude that you have what it takes to deal with anything that life throws at you.

13. **Keep Up Your Enthusiasm.** Enthusiastic people have a great attitude toward life. Have a list of ways to lift your enthusiasm ready for those times when you feel your zest for life draining away. Being enthusiastic will help you maintain the attitude that life is good and that you're lucky to be alive.

14. **Give Up On Having An Attitude of Entitlement.** Think of the parable "Who Moved My Cheese?" by Spencer Johnson. Two little mice and two miniature people are put in a maze. Here's what happens:
    - When the mice discover that the cheese isn't where it's supposed to be, they
    - immediately get to work on finding another piece of cheese.
    - The two miniature people, instead, get angry that the cheese has been moved. They waste time expressing outrage and blaming each other.

    Stop demanding that things be handed to you. Your attitude at all times should be the following:
    - It's up to me to get what I want.
    - Good things come to those who work hard.
    - I adapt to change easily and quickly.
    - I keep going even when things get tough.

15. **Visualize.** When things aren't going your way, keep a positive attitude by visualizing yourself succeeding and achieving your goals. When Nelson Mandela was incarcerated—in a tiny cell that was just 6 feet wide—he kept his hopes up by visualizing himself being set free.

    Mandela once said, "I thought of the day when I would walk free. Over and over again, I fantasized about what I would like to do." By visualizing his release, he was able to maintain a positive attitude, even when he found himself under extraordinarily difficult circumstances.

16. **Limit Your Complaints.** Whining about anything and everything is not conducive to a positive attitude. When you complain, you're saying negative things about a person, place, or event, without offering a solution to fix the situation. Instead of complaining, do the following:
    - Remove yourself from the situation.
    - Shift your perspective about the situation.
    - Offer a possible solution.
    - Accept that there's nothing you can do to change the situation and that complaining about it just fosters negativity.

    Constant complaining leads to a bad attitude. So, stop complaining. Instead, start looking for solutions or accept what cannot be changed.

17. **Watch Your Words.** Use positive words when you talk to yourself. Studies have found that positive self-talk can boost your willpower and help you psych yourself up when you need to get through a difficult task. In addition, it can calm you down when you're worried or anxious.

    If you want to change your attitude from "I can't do this" or "I'm going to fail," to "I've got this" or "I'm going to do great," change your self-talk.

18. **Use The Power of Humor.** People who know how to laugh at themselves and at life's absurdities have a great attitude. Your sense of humor is a powerful tool, and you can use it to lift your mood and enhance your emotional state at any time.

    When something goes wrong, ask yourself, "What's funny about this?" A humorous perspective will have a positive effect on your attitude.

19. **Use Gratitude to Improve Your Attitude.** When you find yourself focusing on what's wrong in your life, what you don't have, or what you're missing out on, adjust your attitude by feeling gratitude.

    Studies show that having an attitude of gratitude is beneficial for every aspect of your life: being grateful improves your health, your mood, your relationships, your career satisfaction, and on and on. If you need an attitude lift, simply think of all the things that you have to be grateful for.

20. **Develop an Attitude of Curiosity.** The best way to approach any situation is to be open to what you can learn from it. That is, be curious.

    Curiosity gives you a present-moment orientation, which is similar to mindfulness. Being curious about a situation allows you to experience it more fully. In addition, curiosity will help you to approach uncertainty in your daily life with a positive attitude.

21. **Seek Out Others With a Positive Attitude.** A positive attitude is contagious. When you feel that you need an attitude boost, find someone with a great attitude and look for an excuse to hang out with them. Their attitude can't help but rub off on you, and you'll be able to face the world with renewed optimism.

DOING YOUR DREAMS

"Do you want to know who you are? Don't ask. ACT! Action will delineate and define you."
– Thomas Jefferson

- It is what you do that defines you
- Don't overthink – Do!
- Don't over-plan and under-act.
- Inaction is expensive
- "Small deeds done are better than great deeds planned" – *Peter Marshall*
- Avoid procrastination, which prevents you from ever reaching your destination
- Do something that moves you forward; even a small act is significant
- Begin by taking small steps towards achieving your goal

It is said that the wealthiest place on earth is the graveyard because people died with unfulfilled dreams, because they didn't "act" on their dreams. A dream is just a day or nighttime wish until you, through intentionality, make it happen. Yes, it takes time and even some moments of what looks like failure. But even those moments are stepping stones to doing better, being better, and having more. Don't just talk about it… BE about it!

The key factor in your success as you move towards your dreams is self-confidence. If you don't believe in yourself, how can you expect others to believe in you?

"Change will not come if we wait for some other person or some other time. We are the ones we've been waiting for. We are the change that we seek." – *President Barack Obama*

RATE YOUR LEVEL OF SELF-CONFIDENCE *(10 being the highest)*	1	2	3	4	5	6	7	8	9	10
I act with self-confidence										
I dress with self-confidence										
I speak assertively										
I think and act positively										
I take action when necessary										
I am always prepared thru planning										

RESUME WRITING

WHAT IS A RESUME?

The resume is a snapshot and showcase of your skills, experiences, and accomplishments that serve as a marketing tool to get you in the door for the interview. All an employer knows about you is what is on your resume - it must be the best reflection of you possible. Remember: "First Impressions are lasting impressions."

TYPES OF RESUMES

Depending on the type of job you are applying to, different resume formats may apply. The four standard types of resumes include 1) chronological, 2) functional, 3) combination, or 4) targeted. Below are definitions of each type and recommendations on which format works best.

Chronological:

- **What is it** - Chronological resumes are the most commonly used format. They list work history in chronological order, starting with your most recent job down to your earliest. This resume is preferred by most employers because it provides a quick snapshot of work history, with the most recent positions up front.
- **Who should use** - If you have a solid work history, your experience is aligned with the job you are applying to, and you have no lapses between employment, use this format.

Functional Resume:

- **What is it** - Unlike chronological resumes, functional resumes focus on your skills and experience first. This type of resume deemphasizes the dates in which you have worked. Employment history is secondary and is listed under the details of your skills.

- **Who should use it** - If you have lapses in employment, are in the middle of a career transition, are a recent college grad with limited work experience, or have a diverse background with no clear career path, this is the most effective type of resume.

Combination Resume:

- **What is it** - Combination resumes let you detail both your skills and experience, while also backing this up with a chronological listing of work history. Flexible in nature, the combination resume lets you tailor to the prospective job opening and tell hiring managers a story.

- **Who should use** - Use this resume if you want to detail work experience to show hiring managers the type of employee you are.

Targeted Resume:

- **What is it** - Targeted resumes are customized in detail to the prospective job you are seeking. Everything from your objective, your qualifications, to your educational experience mirrors the job requirements.

- **Who should use** - These resumes are the most time-consuming, but can generate the best results as the qualifications and experience you outline mirror the prospective job opening closely. Be careful, however, when you develop a targeted resume, you need to be as accurate as possible and not embellish career highlights simply to mirror the job.

> What type of resume is best suited for the job for which you are applying?

FORMAT
- Organized and professional
- Consistent font type
- Appropriate font sizes
- Sections easily identified and placed in the best order
- Appropriate margins
- Void of unnecessary symbols/designs
- Limited use of bullets, bolding, and underlines
- Reversed chronologically listing of work experiences
- 2-page limit
- Omission of unnecessary subtitles (i.e., objective, references, etc.)

WRITING STYLE
- Omission of personal pronouns
- Logical content flow and easy to understand
- Free of typos, spelling, grammar, or syntax errors
- Proofread by others
- Use of strong, varied, and relevant action words
- Includes information relevant to the job for the job being applied

ACCOMPLISHMENTS

- Brief in description
- Quantified using numbers, percentages, and dollar amounts as measures of success
- Relevant to job applied for
- Void of use of abbreviations or acronyms without spelling out
- Void of names of individuals worked for or with

BUILDING AN EFFECTIVE RESUME

HEADING

- Verify that your name and contact information are correct and properly positioned. NOTE: Mailing address can be optional, but is not recommended. However, email addresses and phone numbers are always important. A LinkedIn link can also be included.
- Use a personal email, not one from work.
- Make sure your email address is professional (do not use email addresses such as hotstuff4u@yahoo.com or bigdaddy17@hotmail.com)

QUALIFICATION SUMMARY

- List "what" skills you have to offer that make you compatible for the job for which you are applying. Use bullets and brief sentences.
- Use soft skills and hard skills (core qualifications)
    - Soft skills include attitude, communication, creative thinking, work ethics, teamwork, networking, decision making, positivity, time management, motivation, flexibility, problem-solving, critical thinking, and conflict resolution.

- Hard skills are acquired through formal education and training programs, including college, apprenticeships, short-term training classes, online courses, certification programs, as well as by on-the-job training.

- Titles for this section can vary – "Professional Summary," "Skill Summary," "Core Qualifications."

> List your soft skills. Include those characteristics that you demonstrate in the workplace towards your work, other people, everyday life.
>
>
>
> Now list your hard skills. Include any education, training, certification, relative courses/classes.

EDUCATION
- List education in reverse chronological order (if dates are included), beginning with the most recent educational institution first.
    - Name of educational institution followed by city and state
    - Name of degree (do not use abbreviations or acronyms), i.e., Bachelor of Arts in Business Administration instead of BBA.
    - List only the month and year of completion or the expected date of completion if still pursuing *(optional)*
    - Do not list a high school diploma or GED unless you have not completed or begun completing education beyond high school.

EXPERIENCE
- Be mindful to extend job history for no more than 10 to 12 years unless previous jobs are extremely relevant to the job for which you are applying.
- List job history in reverse chronological order, beginning with the most recent job first.
    o Name of employer and city/state
    o Date of employment
    o Job title
    o Brief, bulleted description of job duties
- If job history includes more than one industry, you may consider grouping those according to the industry, i.e., management, clerical, education, etc.
- List those jobs that are part-time, volunteer, or internships after full-time employment so as to cover any employment gaps or shore up experiences in a particular field of employment (dates are optional)

For each job you list under "Experience," what were your specific duties, quantifiable achievements, and successes? If additional space is needed, use separate sheets.

JOB #1

JOB #2

JOB #3

AFFILIATIONS/HONORS/AWARDS

- List only those affiliations/honors/awards that are relevant to the job(s) for which you intend to apply.
- If using acronyms or abbreviations, list the title followed by the acronyms or abbreviations.
- Dates are not necessary.

What are the names of affiliations (groups or organizations) you are a part of that may be of interest to an employer?

What honors and/or awards have you received within the last 10 years that are specific to the job for which you are applying?

NOTE:

Whereas there is no one format that fits every job search, having the basic knowledge of what should be included on a resume is most important. For each job applied, be sure to tailor your resume according to the job description, using key words that are included in the job description. A good source to assist in finding these words can be found at www.wordle.net. Also, the use of a thesaurus is an excellent source to find action words that are synonymous with less powerful words.

COVER LETTER

WHAT IS A COVER LETTER?

Before you start writing a cover letter, you should familiarize yourself with the document's purpose. A cover letter is a document sent with your resume to provide additional information on your skills and experience. ***A well-written cover letter will help get your application noticed and help you secure an interview. Take the time to personalize it so it shows the employer why you're a solid candidate for the job.***

The letter provides detailed information on why you are qualified for the job you are applying for. Don't simply repeat what's on your resume -- rather, include specific information on why you're a strong match for the employer's job requirements. Think of your cover letter as a sales pitch that will market your credentials and help you get the interview. As such, you want to make sure your cover letter makes the best impression on the person who is reviewing it.

A cover letter typically accompanies each resume you send out. Employers use cover letters as a way to screen applicants for available jobs and to determine which candidates they would like to interview. If an employer requires a cover letter, it will be listed in the job posting. Even if the company doesn't ask for one, you may want to include one anyway.

THE DIFFERENT TYPES OF COVER LETTERS

There are three general types of cover letters. Choose the type of letter that matches your reason for writing.

- The **application letter** which responds to a known job opening (*see cover letter samples*)
- The **prospecting letter** which inquires about possible positions (*see inquiry letter samples*)
- The **networking letter** which requests information and assistance in your job search (*see networking letter examples*)

When you are applying for a job that has been posted by a company that's hiring, you will be using the "application letter" style.

> What type of cover letter do you need?

WHAT TO INCLUDE IN YOUR COVER LETTER

A cover letter should complement, not duplicate, your resume. Its purpose is to interpret the data-oriented, factual resume and add a personal touch to your application for employment. Find out more about the differences between a resume and a cover letter to make sure you start writing your cover letter with the correct approach.

A cover letter is often your earliest written contact with a potential employer, creating a critical first impression. Something that might seem like a small error, like a typo, can get your application immediately knocked off the list. On the other hand, even if your cover letter is error-free and perfectly written, if it is generic (and makes no reference to the company or to any specifics in the job description), it is also likely to be rejected by a hiring manager.

Effective cover letters explain the reasons for your interest in the specific organization and identify your most relevant skills or experiences. Determine relevance by carefully reading the job description, evaluating the skills required, and matching them to your own skills.

Think of instances where you applied those skills, and how you would be effective in the position available.

Review a list of what to include in a cover letter for a job before you get started.

WHAT TO LEAVE OFF YOUR COVER LETTER

There are some things that you don't need to include in the cover letters you write. The letter is about your qualifications for the job, not about you personally. There is no need to share any personal information about yourself or your family in it. If you don't have all the qualifications the employer is seeking, don't mention it. Instead, focus on the credentials you have that are a match. Don't mention salary unless the company asks for your salary requirements. If you have questions about the job, the salary, the schedule, or the benefits, it's not appropriate to mention them in the letter.

One thing that's very important is not to write too much. Keep your letter focused, concise, and a few paragraphs in length. It's important to convey just enough information to entice the hiring manager to contact you for an interview.

If you write too much, it's probably not going to be read.

CUSTOMIZE YOUR COVER LETTER

It is very important that your cover letter be tailored to each position you are applying to. This means more than just changing the name of the company in the body of the letter.

Each cover letter you write should be customized to include:

- Which job you're applying for *(include the job title in your opening paragraph)*
- How you learned about the job *(and a referral if you have one)*
- Why you are qualified for the job *(be specific)*
- What you have to offer the employer, and why you want to work at this specific company *(match your skills to the job description, and read up on the organization's mission, values, and goals to mention in your letter)*
- Thank you for being considered for the job.

To whom does the cover letter need to be addressed? Include name and title.

What is the position you are applying for? Looking for?

How did you learn of the position (if applicable)?

Why are you interested in this job?

Why are you qualified for the job?

What skills (per the job description) do you bring to the job?

COVER LETTER WRITING GUIDELINES

Here's an outline of the items that should be included in every cover letter. Before you get started, it can be helpful to review some cover letter samples, just so you have a visual of how everything fits on the page.

These cover letter examples, both written and email, are designed for a variety of different types of job applications and employment inquiries. Do be sure to take the time to personalize your letter, so it's a strong endorsement of your ability to do the job for which you're applying.

Header
A cover letter should begin with both your and the employer's contact information (name, address, phone number, email), followed by the date. If this is an email rather than an actual letter, include your contact information at the end of the letter, after your signature.

Your contact information should include:
First and Last Name
Street Address
City, State, Zip
Phone
Email

Salutation
Begin your cover letter salutation with "Dr./Mr./Ms. Last Name." If you are unsure if your contact is male or female, you can write out their full name. If you do not know the employer's name, simply write, "Dear Hiring Manager." This is better than the generic and formal, "To Whom It May Concern."

Review information on how to choose the right cover letter greeting to select one that works for the job and company you're applying to.

Introduction
Begin your introduction by stating what job you are applying for. Explain where you heard about the job, particularly if you heard about it from a contact associated with the company. Briefly mention how your skills and experience match the company and/or position; this will give the employer a preview of the rest of your letter. Your goal in the introduction is to get the reader's attention. To get started, see examples of engaging opening sentences for cover letters.

Body
In a paragraph or two, explain why you are interested in the job and why you make an excellent candidate for the position. Mention specific qualifications listed in the job posting and explain how you

meet those qualifications. Do not simply restate your resume, but provide specific examples that demonstrate your abilities. Remember, actions speak louder than words, so don't just "tell" the reader that you are, for example, a great team player with strong communication skills and an excellent attention to detail. Instead, use tangible examples from your work experience to "show" these traits in action. Here's more information on what to include in the body section of a cover letter.

Closing

In the closing section of your cover letter, restate how your skills make you a strong fit for the company and/or position. If you have room (remember, just like your resume, your cover letter should be no longer than one page - here's more information on how long a cover letter should be), you can also discuss why you would like to work at that specific company.

State that you would like the opportunity to interview or discuss employment opportunities. Explain what you will do to follow up, and when you will do it. Thank the employer for his/her consideration.

Signature

Use a complimentary close, and then end your cover letter with your signature, handwritten, followed by your typed name. If this is an email, simply include your typed name, followed by your contact information, after the complimentary close.

FORMAT YOUR COVER LETTER

Your cover letter should be formatted like a professional business letter. The font should match the font you used on your resume and should be simple and easy to read. Basic fonts like Arial, Calibri, Georgia, Verdana, and Times New Roman work well. A font size of 10 or 12 points is easy to read. Standard margins are 1" on the top, bottom, and left and right sides of the page.

Add a space between the header, salutation, each paragraph, the closing, and your signature. You can reduce the font and margin sizes to keep your document on a single page but do be sure to leave enough white space for your letter to be easy to read.

Follow these cover letter formatting guidelines to ensure your letters match the professional standards expected by the hiring managers who review applications.

EDIT AND PROOFREAD YOUR COVER LETTER

Remember to edit and proofread your cover letter before sending it. It may sound silly, but make sure you include the correct employer and company names - when you write multiple cover letters at once, it is easy to make a mistake. Printing out and reading the letter aloud is a good way to catch small typos, such as missing words or sentences that sound odd.

Always double-check the spelling of your contact's name, as well as the company name. Here are more tips for proofreading a cover letter. If possible, enlist a friend or a family member to help proofread your cover letter, as two pairs of eyes are better than one, and even professional proofreaders don't always catch their own mistakes.

WHAT IS A THANK YOU LETTER?

A thank-you letter is sent as a courtesy to employers, usually following an interview, typically within 24 hours of the interview.

Thank You Letter Format
- For header and salutation, follow the same guidelines as for the cover letter.
- Thank the interviewer, highlight your qualifications, and express interest in the job if indeed interested. If not, simply thank them.
- Include and highlight something you may have forgotten to state in the interview.
- Place phone number near the end, even though it's also at the top.
- Sign both your first and last name.
- Proofread multiple times and then ask someone else to proofread as well.

INTERVIEW SKILLS

A job interview is a one-on-one interview consisting of a conversation between a job applicant and a representative of an employer, which is conducted to assess whether the applicant should be hired. Interviews are one of the most popularly used devices for employee selection.

Every employer has a preferred style of obtaining the information they need for their hiring decision. These are some basic types of interview styles you may encounter. Some employers may choose to utilize a combination of different styles, but as long as you've prepared well for your interview, you'll be able to adapt to the situation they present.

TYPES OF JOB INTERVIEWS

Structured Interview

A structured interview is typically formal and organized, and may include several interviewers, commonly referred to as a panel interview. An interviewer who has a more structured style will usually begin with what is known as an "icebreaker" question. The icebreaker is used to relax you before the more serious questions are asked. A discussion about the weather might be used, or perhaps a question about the traffic on your way to the office.

Next, the interviewer may talk for a few minutes about the company and the position. During this time, the interviewer may describe the day-to-day work responsibilities and the general company philosophy. He or she may then ask you a series of questions regarding your past educational, co-curricular, and work experiences.

Finally, the interviewer may ask if you have questions for him or her. You should always have several questions prepared. This type of interview is structured and formal.

Unstructured Interview

The unstructured interview is what the name implies. The only structure to the interview is the one that you provide. Basically, the interviewer is interested in hearing from you, so you may be asked a variety of different open-ended questions.

You will find an unstructured interview to be more conversational and less formal in tone than a structured interview. You may be asked questions about your hobbies, what you do on the weekends, or other casual questions designed to put you at ease. Many students prefer this laid-back style of interviewing, but you must be cautious. Sometimes employers intentionally adopt this casual demeanor so that you feel comfortable enough to let down your guard and potentially reveal something that you normally would not. If you find yourself in an unstructured interview, be friendly but maintain your professionalism. Remember that you are there to showcase your best assets and to convince the employer that you are the most qualified candidate for the job. Casual conversation is acceptable, and it can set a positive tone for the interview, but be sure to bring the conversation around to your skills and qualifications.

Stress Interview

This style is used primarily by interviewers who are hiring for positions where there is a high level of daily stress in the work environment (i.e., sales, stockbroker, etc.).

The same questions that are asked during a structured or unstructured interview may be asked for a stress interview. However, there may be a difference in the behavior or demeanor of the interviewer. The interviewer during a stress interview may appear distracted, contrary, or indifferent to you. The idea behind this type of interview is to assess your reaction to the pressure of indifference, rejection, and overall stress. To be successful in the stress interview, it is recommended that you focus on the question that is asked and not the manner in which it is asked.

Another hallmark of a stress interview is the "strange question." For instance, some interviewers like to ask questions such as, "How many ping pong balls can fit in a 757 jet?" To answer a question like this, break it down into smaller, more manageable components. Verbally convey your decision-making process. The interviewer will be less focused on whether or not you came to the "right" answer and more focused on your ability to problem-solve and think logically.

Sometimes in a stress interview, the interviewer will put candidates in an uncomfortable situation. For instance, candidates may be given a test that takes two hours to complete and are told to complete it in thirty minutes. Remember to stay calm throughout a stress interview, because that is what the employer is looking for – a candidate who has the ability to remain cool, calm, and collected.

Behavioral Interview

Behavioral interviewing is a widely used method of job interviewing. This approach is based on the belief that past performance is the best predictor of future behavior. Therefore, behavioral interview questions are designed to probe your previous experiences in order to determine how you might behave in similar situations in the future. In this type of interview, you will not be asked hypothetical questions about how you would handle a situation if confronted with it in the future. Instead, you will be asked how you handled a specific situation when you encountered it in the past. Keep in mind that employers are not interested in what you should have done, or what you will do next time...they want to know what you actually did. Behavioral interview questions generally start with any one of the following phrases:

- Tell me about a time when you...
- Describe a circumstance when you were faced with a problem related to...
- Tell me how you approached a situation where...
- Share with me an instance in which you demonstrated...

This type of question requires you to tell stories from your past. These stories will be evaluated for evidence of your intellectual competence, leadership, teamwork, personal skills, adjustment and flexibility, motivation, communication skills, administrative skills, and technical abilities.

To prepare for a behavioral interview, you must first identify the skills and strengths that the employer is seeking. Next, reflect on your past experiences (educational, employment, extra-curricular, and personal) in order to identify situations in which you clearly demonstrated the identified skills. During the interview, you must be able to recount these circumstances articulately and in a manner that showcases your strengths. A thorough answer should describe the Situation, the Tasks with which you were charged, the Action you took, and the Result of your action. We refer to this as the STAR Method of responding to behavioral interview questions.

Panel Interview

Employers often like to gather the opinions of several members of their staff prior to deciding which candidate to hire. To accomplish this, panel interviews are often used, where one candidate may be interviewed by a few people at once. In a panel interview, take note of each interviewer's name and refer to them by their names. When giving your answers, focus on the person who asked you the question, but make eye contact with the other members of the group from time to time. Panel interviews can vary in style and tone, but generally, they will be more formal and include behavior-based questions.

Screening Interview

A screening interview is a type of job interview that is conducted to determine if the applicant has the qualifications needed to do the job for which the company is hiring. A screening interview is typically the first interview in the hiring process if the company does not start with open interviews, where multiple candidates are screened at an open hiring event.   Interviewers are looking to see if you

have the necessary skills for the position and if your salary expectations match the budget allocated for the role. Typical questions during a screening interview include:
- Tell me about yourself.
- Describe your work history.
- What are your salary requirements?
- Why are you interested in this job?
- Specific skill-based questions, e.g., Have you worked deploying newsletters? Do you have experience setting up successful store displays?

Phone Interview

Employers use phone interviews to identify and recruit candidates for employment. Phone interviews are often used to narrow the pool of applicants who will be invited for in-person interviews. For remote jobs, interviewing by phone, Skype, or video may be how you get hired.

Virtual Interview

Since and during COVID, virtual interviewing has become extremely popular. Virtual interviewing is a remote job interview conducted through online platforms like Zoom, Microsoft Teams, or Google Meet. It allows employers and candidates to connect virtually, often as a first or final interview step. It tests not only qualifications but also professionalism, communication, and comfort with technology.

Group Interview

You might also have a group interview, in which you are either interviewed by a panel or interviewed along with a group of candidates. For this kind of interview, you want to practice both answering questions and being a good listener (which you can show by responding thoughtfully to your group members' comments and through your body language).

Make sure you know what kind of interview you will be having before you arrive. If you are unsure, do not hesitate to ask the employer or recruiter who set up the meeting.

Dining Interview

Dining with a job applicant allows the employer to review your communication and interpersonal skills, as well as your table manners, in a more relaxed (for them) environment. Depending on the interview process of the company you're interviewing with and the type of job you are applying for, you may be invited to a lunch or dinner interview. Table manners do matter. Good manners may give you the edge over another candidate, so take some time to brush up on your dining etiquette skills.

> What style/type of interview will you be attending?

JOB INTERVIEW ETIQUETTE (In Person)

BE ON TIME
- Being on time for an interview is an employer's perspective regarding your time management and work ethic. If you can't be prompt for an interview, what are the odds that you will be at work on time or finish projects on time?
- It's important to arrive a few minutes early, or on time, at the latest, for a job interview. Know where you're going, how much travel time you need, and how to get to the interview location. Check out the logistics ahead of time so you ensure that you're not late.
- Giving yourself a bit of extra time will give you an opportunity to stop in the restroom and freshen up, if need be, to make sure you don't have any hair, make-up, or wardrobe malfunctions.
- A few extra minutes will also give you an opportunity to catch your breath and stay calm. An interview is even more stressful than normal if you're rushing to get there on time.

- **WHAT TO BRING TO A JOB INTERVIEW**
- **Do:**
  - Bring extra copies of your resume along with a list of references.
  - Bring a list of questions to ask the interviewer.
  - Bring examples of your work (if job requires)
  - Turn off the cell phone and put it out of sight (purse, pocket, etc.)
- **Don't:**
  - Bring coffee cup or bottle of soda or water or anything to eat or drink.
  - Chew gum

> What items will you take to the interview?

WHAT TO WEAR TO AN INTERVIEW

A big part of getting a job is making a good first impression, and a big part of **making a good first impression** is how you dress for the interview. While you don't have to spend a lot of money on your wardrobe, putting in a little extra effort will pay off in the long run. Before your next interview, make sure you aren't making any interview attire mistakes.

- **COLORS:**
  - Solids rather than patterns
  - Neutrals rather than brights
  - **Brown** - Brown is a neutral color that evokes feelings of calm. It is a great, solid, neutral color for any interview.
  - **Blue** - Blue, particularly navy, is another great neutral color for interview outfits. Blues convey feelings of calm, trust, and confidence - great qualities for an interviewer to sense in you. Darker blues (like navy) convey authority and confidence. Blue is also many people's favorite color, and wearing an interviewer's favorite color will always make a great first impression.
  - **Gray** - Gray is another great neutral color for interview outfits. It evokes sophistication and neutrality. Gray is a great color to wear as a suit or dress; it allows you to look powerful but is not quite as domineering as a black suit or dress.
  - **Black** - Black is a very popular color for suits and dresses in interviews. However, black is a very commanding color that conveys a lot of power, authority, and even drama. This is a good color for a job in a conservative environment like a law office, or for an interviewee applying for a high-level executive position. However, black can be a bit overwhelming in a more laid-back office environment and can make you appear unapproachable. Using black as an accent color (for example, in a scarf or tie) can give you a bit of that sense of authority without being overwhelming.
  - **Red** - Red is a bright, powerful color that conveys energy and passion. A pop of red (for example, in a scarf or tie) can convey just the right amount of passion without making you appear too emotional.
  - **White** - Crisp and clean, white is a great color for shirts and blouses. The color conveys truth and simplicity and adds a bit of brightness without being too overwhelming.

PROFESSIONAL MEN'S ATTIRE
- Suit (solid color - navy, black, or dark grey)
- Long-sleeved shirt (white or coordinated with the suit)
- Belt
- Tie (here's how to tie it)
- Dark socks, conservative leather shoes
- Little or no jewelry
- Neat, professional hairstyle

- Limit the aftershave.
- Neatly trimmed nails
- Portfolio or briefcase

PROFESSIONAL WOMEN'S ATTIRE

In general, fashion for women is more complicated and varied, which makes assembling an interview outfit a bit more challenging for women than it is for men. For instance, for any job interview where a woman is wearing a dress or skirt, she needs to determine if she should wear pantyhose or if bare legs are acceptable. Women also need to consider interview accessories and choose an appropriate purse, options that are professional, large enough to fit a resume, and aren't flashy.

- Suit (navy, black, or dark grey) - make sure the suit's skirt is long enough so you can sit down comfortably.
- Coordinated blouse
- Conservative shoes
- Limited jewelry (no dangling earrings or arms full of bracelets)
- No jewelry is better than cheap jewelry.
- Professional hairstyle
- Neutral pantyhose
- Light make-up and perfume
- Neatly manicured, clean nails
- Portfolio or briefcase

BUSINESS CASUAL ATTIRE BASICS

Women

- Women should wear a combination of a skirt or dress slacks, blouse, sweater, twinset, jacket (optional), and hosiery (optional) with closed-toe shoes. Sandals or peep-toe shoes may be permissible in some offices; flip-flops are never considered part of business casual.
- Khaki, corduroy, twill, or cotton pants or skirts (skirts should not be short)
- Sweaters, twinsets, cardigans, polo/knit shirts
- A sheath dress is often flattering and looks very professional.
- Solid colors work better than bright patterns.

Men

- For men, appropriate business casual attire is dress slacks or chinos, a shirt with or without a tie, dark socks, and dress shoes. Avoid wearing polo shirts to an interview, even if they are acceptable for the job in question.
- Do not wear jeans or shorts.
- Khaki, gabardine, wool, or cotton pants, neatly pressed
- Cotton long-sleeved button-down shirts, pressed
- Sweaters
- Leather shoes and belt
- Tie optional

WHAT NOT TO WEAR TO AN INTERVIEW

- short hemlines and plunging necklines
- bright, flashy colors
- short hemlines and skin-tight fits
- V-neck blouses
- t-shirt
- loud or excessive amounts of perfume/cologne
- excessive makeup (dark eye shadow, bright lipstick, heavy foundation)
- headphones
- shorts
- tank top
- skimpy sundress
- jeans
- outdated clothing
- sneakers
- sandals
- open-toed shoes
- worn-out shoes
- tacky or novelty ties (i.e., Christmas, American flag, music, etc.)
- excess jewelry (big hoops or chandelier earrings, flashy necklaces or watches, cufflinks, tie clips, belts, bracelets)
- shades (on your eyes or head)

Describe what you will wear to the interview:

DURING THE INTERVIEW

- Say the name of the person you are greeting. It sounds polite and friendly – and people like hearing their own name. But remember, only address the interviewer by his or her first name if they invite you to.
- Don't forget to smile and make eye contact with the interviewer!
- Do not sit until and unless you are invited to do so.
- Present with good energy.
- Keep your movements smooth and avoid fidgeting.
- Keep your posture open at all times. Crossed arms suggest a closed and defensive position.
- Make sure your hands are comfortably rested one on top of the other, or one on the arm of the chair, and the other one in your lap.
- Do not prop your chin with your elbow on the interviewer's desk or table where you are sitting.
- A big factor in how well you interview is your nonverbal communication. That includes your **posture, your body language,** and, perhaps most important, your **eye contact.** Appropriate **eye contact** speaks to confidence and self-esteem – important assets in any good employee.
- Once the interview is finished, do not stand to exit until the interviewer has stood.
- End the interview with a thank you statement, a smile, and a firm handshake.

PHONE INTERVIEW ETIQUETTE

Get Ready for the Call

Before the call, confirm all the details, including the date, time, and who you will be talking to. Be sure you know whether the interviewer is calling you or if you need to make the call.
Use a quiet, comfortable, and private space with no distractions so you can focus on the interview.

Follow these tips for a successful phone interview:

- Keep your resume in clear view, on the top of your desk, or tape it to the wall near the phone, so it's at your fingertips when you need to answer questions.
- Have a short list of your accomplishments available to review.
- Have a pen and paper handy for note-taking.
- Turn call-waiting off, so your call isn't interrupted.
- If the time isn't convenient, ask if you could talk at another time and suggest some alternatives.
- Clear the room — evict the kids and the pets. Turn off the stereo and the TV. Close the door.
- If you have a landline, use that instead of your cell phone. That way, you'll eliminate the possibility of poor reception or dropped calls.

Do's and Don'ts During the Phone Interview

- **Don't** smoke, chew gum, eat, or drink.
- **Do** keep a glass of water handy in case you need to wet your mouth.
- **Do** smile. Smiling will project a positive image to the listener and will change the tone of your voice. It can also be helpful to stand during the interview since this typically gives your voice more energy and enthusiasm.
- **Do** speak slowly and enunciate clearly.
- **Do** use the person's title (Mr. or Ms. and their last name.) Only use their first name if they ask you to.
- **Don't** interrupt the interviewer.
- **Do** take your time — it's perfectly acceptable to take a moment or two to collect your thoughts.
- **Do** take notes when possible on what questions came up.
- **Do** give short answers.
- **Do** remember your goal is to set up a face-to-face interview. At the end of your conversation, after you thank the interviewer, ask if it would be possible to meet in person.

VIRTUAL INTERVIEW ETIQUETTE

- **Dress for Success**
    - Wear professional or business-casual attire (as if in person)
    - Choose solid, neutral colors - avoid bright or patterned clothing
    - Ensure clothing is clean, pressed, and fits well
    - Keep accessories, jewelry, and makeup simple and professional
    - Groom nearly (hair, facial hair, etc.)
- **Set Up Your Background**
    - Choose a clean, quiet, and uncluttered space
    - Use a neutral wall or tidy office area
    - Remove distractions (personal items, posters, etc.)
    - Use a neutral virtual background only if your real space isn't suitable
    - Position the camera at eye level for a natural view
- **Perfect Your Lighting**
    - Sit facing a window or light source for even lighting
    - Avoid light behind you (it creates shadows)
    - Use a ring light or desk lamp if natural light is low
    - Make sure your face is well-lit and visible on camera

- **Technology Check**
    - Test your camera, microphone, and internet connection
    - Charge your device or keep it plugged in
    - Log in 5-10 minutes early to check settings
    - Close unnecessary apps or browser tabs
- **Other Tips**
    - Maintain eye contact by looking into the camera
    - Smile and use confident body language
    - Keep notes nearby but avoid reading from them
    - Eliminate background noise (mute phones, pets, etc.)
    - Send a thank-you message after the interview

DINING INTERVIEW ETIQUETTE

- Are you really nervous? Check out the restaurant ahead of time. That way, you'll know exactly what's on the menu, what you might want to order, and where the restrooms are located.
- Be polite. Remember to say "please" and "thank you" to your server as well as to your host.
- Is the table full of utensils? My British grandmother taught me an easy way to remember what to use when. Start at the outside and work your way in. Your salad fork will be on the far left, and your entree fork will be next to it. Your dessert spoon and fork will be above your plate.
- Liquids are on the right, solids on the left. For example, your water glass will be on the right and your bread plate will be on the left.
- Put your napkin on your lap once everyone is seated.
- Remember what your mother spent years telling you - keep your elbows off the table, sit up straight, and don't talk with your mouth full!

During the Meal:

- Don't order messy food - pasta with lots of sauce, chicken with bones, ribs, big sandwiches, and whole lobsters are all dangerous.
    - Don't order the most expensive entree on the menu.
    - Do order food that is easy to cut into bite-sized pieces.
- The polite way to eat soup is to spoon it away from you. There's less chance of spilling in your lap that way, too!
    - Break your dinner roll into small pieces and eat it a piece at a time.
- If you need to leave the table, put your napkin on the seat or the arm of your chair.
- When you've finished eating, move your knife and fork to the "four o'clock" position so the server knows you're done.
    - Remember to try and relax, listen, and participate in the conversation.

To Drink or Not to Drink:

- It's wise not to drink alcohol during an interview. Interviewing is tough enough without adding alcohol to the mix.

After the Meal:

- Put your napkin on the table next to your plate.
- Let the prospective employer pick up the tab. The person who invited you will expect to pay both the bill and the tip.
- Remember to say, "thank you." Consider also following up with a thank-you note, which reiterates your interest in the job.

BASIC JOB INTERVIEW QUESTIONS

LEGAL VS. ILLEGAL AREAS OF INQUIRY

While some information can be elicited once you have been hired, government legislation exists that discourages employers from asking certain questions during the interview process. Technically, employers can ask any questions they want to; they just cannot use certain information in making hiring decisions. In order to avoid potential problems, employers typically avoid certain topics. Some of these discouraged areas of inquiry include:

- Age
- Race
- Religion
- National origin (an employer can, however, ask if you are legally able to work in the U.S.)
- Sex and/or sexual orientation
- Marital status
- If you are asked one of these questions during an interview, very tactfully and professionally say that you are "confident that the area in question (e.g., sex, sexual orientation, age, marital status, etc.) will not adversely affect my ability to do my job and fulfill my responsibilities." You may also choose to ask the interviewer to explain how the question pertains to the job and your ability to fulfill the responsibilities.

TELL ME ABOUT YOURSELF
- When an interviewer says, "Tell me about yourself," the interviewer wants information that is pertinent to the job you're interviewing for.
- The secret to responding to this free-form request successfully is to focus, script, and practice. You cannot afford to wing this answer, as it will affect the rest of the interview. Begin to think about what you want the interviewer to know about you.
- Focus
- List five strengths you have that are pertinent to this job (experiences, traits, skills, etc.). What do you want the interviewer to know about you when you leave?
- EX: strong in communications, connecting with people, strong background, proven success with customer relationships, follow-through, meeting deadlines.
- Follow your script
- Prepare a script that includes the information you want to convey. Begin by talking about past experiences and proven success.
- Next, mention your strengths and abilities.
- Conclude with a statement about your current situation.
- Practice
- Practice with your script until you feel confident about what you want to emphasize in your statement. Your script should help you stay on track, but you shouldn't memorize it—you don't want to sound stiff and rehearsed. It should sound natural and conversational. The more you can talk about your product—you—the better chance you will have at selling it.

Describe and practice what you will say when asked, "Tell me about yourself."

WHAT ARE YOUR STRENGTHS?

Identifying your five key strengths and matching them up with the job requirements is an important step in preparing for your interview. Read through the description and identify the key factors needed to do the job. Be sure to read between the lines.

> What are your areas of strengths?

WHAT ARE YOUR WEAKNESSES?

- This question is asked by employers to assess which areas you feel they need to improve and what you are doing about it. Be up front during interviews. Don't say you have "no weaknesses" or "work too hard." Instead, tell hiring managers what you are working on improving and what you've done to build your skills in these areas.

- One thing to keep in mind: If one of your weaknesses is directly related to the position and could potentially take you out of the running, the opportunity may not be right for you.

> How would you describe your weaknesses?

WHY DO YOU WANT THIS JOB?

Show how your skills match
- At every point of the interview, you need to show your skills and ability to solve problems are a good fit for the company.
- Go back to the job description and your earlier conversations with hiring managers to review what they're looking for and craft your answer around that.

- **Show your enthusiasm for the job**
- Your answer should show that you'll be able to use or learn key skills in the position that are important to you.
- While the question seems to ask about what you want, remember that it's really about the employer. So even as you talk about what has you excited, put it into the context of how this will make you an asset to the organization.
- Find a way to mention your long-term prospects at the company, and you can also quell the employer's concerns about retention or edge out another candidate who might be a flight risk.
- **Show how you fit into the culture**
- The company isn't just interviewing you to find out about your skills. They want to know if you'll be a decent coworker. So, your answer needs to prove that your goals and values are similar to the organization's. Your research for the interview—grilling friends you know who work there and reading up on the latest news about the company—should give you a sense of the firm's mission and values.

WHERE WOULD YOU LIKE TO BE IN YOUR CAREER FIVE YEARS FROM NOW?

- When an interviewer asks you, "Where would you like to be in your career five years from now?" he or she is testing your level of ambition.
- **Explain how your goals align with the company's**
- You say: "I respect how this company develops its employees, and I hope that in five years I'll be managing my own team and helping to expand my department."
- **Show the right amount of ambition**
- Employers want to know their employees have some desire to grow in their careers, Chalmers says. You can include an interest in management training or a desire to work your way into a specific position you have your eye on.
- You say: "I want to explore management training opportunities and also learn the finer points of this industry so I can eventually become a company leader."
- **Show an interest in learning**
- Let's face it, a lot of people don't know exactly what they want to be doing in five years, but you can always express a desire to learn and grow more in a certain area.
- Talk about some aspect of your work life that you'd like to improve. Maybe there's an area of the business that you don't understand and would like to learn more about. Or, maybe there's a new language you'd like to learn or a class you'd like to take. Show them you're interested in knowing more than you do right now.

WHAT ATTRACTED YOU TO THIS COMPANY?

The interviewer is looking for an answer that indicates you've thought about where you want to work—that you're not just sending your resume to any company with a job opening. Researching the company and industry before your interview will make you stand out as a more informed and competent applicant. Search company Websites for mission statements, product and service information, principals' backgrounds, and contact information. Check the company's financials through the US Securities and Exchange Commission. By reviewing the company's website and social media accounts, and reading news articles about the firm, you'll be able to draw conclusions about the value you can bring to the position, whether it's because the company's mission matches yours, its culture is a good fit, or you have a skill that the company needs.

WHY SHOULD WE HIRE YOU?
- **Develop a sales statement**
    - The more detail you give, the better your answer will be. This is not a time to talk about what you want. Rather, it is a time to summarize your accomplishments and relate what makes you unique.
- **Product inventory exercise**
    - The bottom line of this question is, "What can you do for this company?"
    - Start by looking at the job description or posting. What is the employer stressing as requirements of the job? What will it take to get the job done?
- **Make a list of those requirements**
    - Next, do an inventory to determine what you have to offer as a fit for those requirements. Think of two or three key qualities you have to offer that match those the employer is seeking. Don't underestimate personal traits that make you unique; your energy, personality type, working style, and people skills are all very relevant to any job.
- **The sales pitch: You are the solution**
    - From the list of requirements, match what you have to offer and merge the two into a summary statement. This is your sales pitch. It should be no more than two minutes long and should stress the traits that make you unique and a good match for the job.

Describe why an employer should hire you:

WHAT DID YOU LIKE LEAST ABOUT YOUR LAST JOB?

- **Stay on task**
  - When you answer this question, it's best to focus on tasks rather than company politics or people. A good response would be:
  - I've given this question some thought, and overall, I've been very satisfied with my jobs. I've been able to work with some really interesting people. I have to say that I did have a job where there was an inordinate amount of paperwork. Because working with people is my strength, the paperwork really bogged me down at times.
  - Notice the word "inordinate." Not a normal load of paperwork, but an unusually large amount, which kept you from doing what you do best: working with people.

WHY ARE YOU LEAVING YOUR PRESENT JOB?

- **Emphasize results**
  - **Do:** Focus on results: Make a list of things you accomplished in your last position and focus on those, ending with something like, "'Having successfully done that, I'm ready for another challenge,'" "Now what you're saying to the interviewer is: 'You can count on me to get results and stay here until I do.'"
  - **Don't:** Answer in a way that doesn't reassure the interviewer. "Answers such as, 'I wasn't being challenged,' 'The work was no longer interesting,' or 'The pay was too low' all say the same thing to the interviewer: that you might leave at any time if things aren't to your liking."
  - **Recover:** If you give a bland answer, circle back to it quickly. And if you can't, revisit why you left your last job just before you end the interview.
    - This allows you to leave the interviewer with your previous accomplishments top of mind.
  - **Be polite**
  - **Don't** badmouth the boss or the company. That implies you may be difficult to manage.
  - **Don't** dwell too long on your previous employer—the interview is about you, after all.

BEHAVIORAL INTERVIEW QUESTIONS

- **Be sure to include these four points in your answer: situation, task, action, and results.**
- **(S)** A specific situation
- **(T)** The tasks that needed to be done
- **(A)** The action you took
- **(R)** The results, i.e., what happened

- The best behavioral interview strategy includes listening carefully, being clear and detailed when you respond, and, most importantly, being honest. If your answers aren't what the interviewer is looking for, this position may not be the best job for you anyway.
- What was the most difficult period in your life, and how did you deal with it?
- Give me an example of a time you did something wrong. How did you handle it?
- Tell me about a time when you had to deal with conflict on the job.
- If you were at a business lunch and you ordered a rare steak and they brought it to you well done, what would you do?
- If you found out your company was doing something against the law, like fraud, what would you do?
- What assignment was too difficult for you, and how did you resolve the issue?
- What's the most difficult decision you've made in the last two years, and how did you come to that decision?
- Describe how you would handle a situation if you were required to finish multiple tasks by the end of the day, and there was no conceivable way that you could finish them.

Describe a challenge/situation you had on your job using the STAR approach:

SITUATION_____

TASK_____

ACTION_____

RESULT_____

Your opportunity to ask questions usually comes at the end of the interview. You must prepare at least **two or three questions** that demonstrate your interest in the position, your drive to excel in the role, and the fact that you've done some homework (researched the company, industry, department).

Avoid yes or no questions and avoid questions that are so broad that they are difficult to answer. You don't want to stump the interviewer when you're trying to make a good impression and develop rapport.

1. Can you tell me more about the day-to-day responsibilities of this job?
2. What do you think are the most important qualities for someone to excel in this role?
3. What are your expectations for this role during the first 30 days, 60 days, year?
4. Describe the culture of the company.
5. Where do you think the company is headed in the next 5 years?
6. Who do you consider your top competitor, and why?
7. What are the biggest opportunities facing the company/department right now?
8. What are the biggest challenges facing the company/department right now?
9. What do you like best about working for this company?
10. What is the typical career path for someone in this role?
11. How do I compare with the other candidates you've interviewed for this role?
12. What are the next steps in the interview process?

What questions do you have for the employer?

1. _____

2. _____

3. _____

4. _____

NOTE:
Don't ask about salary or benefits just yet. Wait until you are in the final steps of the interview process to negotiate with the hiring manager or an HR representative.

However, you may want to inquire about a salary range prior to the interview. If no one provides you with a salary range before the interview, by all means inquire at the end.

Preparation + Opportunity = SUCCESS

NETWORKING & COMMUNICATION

WHAT IS NETWORKING?

Networking is an important career development skill that is worth developing. In its simplest form, networking involves having a "career conversation" with someone for the purpose of exploring careers or job searching. When you are actively looking for jobs, use networking to market yourself.

Networking is the best way to find a job because:

- People do business primarily with people they know and like. Resumes and cover letters alone are often too impersonal to convince employers to hire you.
- Job listings tend to draw piles of applicants, which puts you in intense competition with many others. Networking makes you a recommended member of a much smaller pool.
- The job you want may not be advertised at all. Networking leads to information and job leads, often before a formal job description is created or a job announced.

OVERCOMING THE FEAR OF NETWORKING

If you're nervous about making contact—either because you're uncomfortable asking for favors or embarrassed about your employment situation—try to keep the following things in mind:

- It feels good to help others. Most people will gladly assist you if they can.
- People like to give advice and be recognized for their expertise.
- Almost everyone knows what it's like to be out of work or looking for a job. They'll
- sympathize with your situation.
    - Unemployment can be isolating and stressful. By connecting with others, you're sure to get some much-needed encouragement, fellowship, and moral support.
- Reconnecting with the people in your network should be fun—even if you have an agenda. The more this feels like a chore, the more tedious and anxiety-ridden the process will be.

Do you engage in frequent networking? If not, what are your networking fears?

WHO ARE YOUR NETWORKS?

- Family
- Friends
- Neighbors
- Co-workers
- Colleagues
- Casual acquaintances
- Fellow civic club members
- Church members
- Former co-workers/supervisors
- Classmates
- Your child's school
- Gym acquaintances/partners
- Friend of a friend
- Doctor
- Landlord
- Banker

List at least 10 networks to which you have access:

FOCUS ON BUILDING RELATIONSHIPS

- **Be authentic.** In any job search or networking situation, being you—the real you—should be your goal. Hiding who you are or suppressing your true interests and goals will only hurt you in the long run. Pursuing what you want and not what you think others will like will always be more fulfilling and ultimately more successful.
- **Be considerate.** If you're reconnecting with an old friend or colleague, take the time to get through the catching-up phase before you blurt out your need. On the other hand, if this person is a busy professional you don't know well, be respectful of his or her time and come straight out with your request.
- **Ask for advice,** not a job. Don't ask for a job; a request comes with a lot of pressure. You want your contacts to become allies in your job search, not make them feel ambushed, so ask for information or insight instead. If they're able to hire you or refer you to someone who can, they will. If not, you haven't put them in the uncomfortable position of turning you down or telling you they can't help.

- **Be specific in your request.** Before you go off and reconnect with everyone you've ever known, get your act together and do a little homework. Be prepared to articulate what you're looking for. Is it a reference? An insider's take on the industry? A referral? An introduction to someone in the field? Also, make sure to provide an update on your qualifications and recent professional experience.

STRENGTHEN & MAINTAIN YOUR JOB NETWORK

Tap into your strong ties

Your strong ties will logically and trustingly lead to new weak ties that build a stronger network. Use your existing network to add members and reconnect with people. Start by engaging the people in your trusted inner circle to help you fill in the gaps in your network.

Think about where you want to go

Your network should reflect where you're going, not just where you've been. Adding people to your network who reflect issues, jobs, industries, and areas of interest is essential. If you are a new graduate or a career changer, join the professional associations that represent your desired career path. Attending conferences, reading journals, and keeping up with the lingo of your desired field can prepare you for where you want to go.

Make the process of connecting a priority

Make connecting a habit—part of your lifestyle. Connecting is just as important as your exercise routine. It breathes life into you and gives you confidence. Find out how your network is doing in this environment, what steps they are taking, and how you can help. As you connect, the world will feel smaller, and a small world is much easier to manage.

Schedule time with your key contacts

List the people who are crucial to your network—people you know who can and have been very important to you. Invariably, there will be some you have lost touch with.
Reconnect and then schedule a regular meeting or phone call. You don't need a reason to get in touch. It will always make you feel good and provide you with an insight or two.

Prioritize the rest of your contacts

Keep a running list of people you need to reconnect with. People whose view of the world you value. People you'd like to get to know better or whose company you enjoy. Prioritize these contacts and then schedule time into your regular routine so you can make your way down the list.

Take notes on the people in your network

Collecting cards and filing them is a start. But maintaining your contacts, new and old, requires updates. Add notes about their families, their jobs, their interests, and their needs. Unless you have a photographic memory, you won't remember all of this information unless you write it down. Put these updates and notes on the back of their business cards or input them into your contact database.

Find ways to reciprocate

Always remember that successful networking is a two-way street. Your ultimate goal is to cultivate mutually beneficial relationships. That means giving as well as receiving.
Send a thank-you note, ask them about their family, email an article you think they might be interested in, and check in periodically to see how they're doing. By nurturing the relationship through your job search and beyond, you'll establish a strong network of people you can count on for ideas, advice, feedback, and support.

STAY ACTIVE

During periods of unemployment, it is good to continue or become active. This not only means being active in your job search but active in your personal, daily life. Consider such activities as:

- Participating in community events
- Attending public conferences or workshops
- Keeping active in and around your home by cleaning the house, washing the car, or tending to the yard and garden
- Working out at a gym or at home using workout videos
- Going hiking or walking in your local area
- Joining and participating in free sports teams or leagues

SOCIAL MEDIA NETWORKING

Social media is at the intersection of technology and human interaction. We are gradually shifting to websites that offer the opportunity for greater human interaction. We leave comments and share information.

Social media is used in a number of ways. It helps recruiters have a clearer idea of who you are and what you have done before they even talk with you. They also pick up clues about your personality and how you might fit into their corporate culture.

In your use of social media, employers and recruiters can see or have an indication of:
- How well you communicate (your spelling, punctuation, and grammar as well as your ability to clearly communicate ideas).
- Your work history and education.
- Your industry knowledge.
- Your use of alcohol.
- Your use of illegal substances.
- Your use of profanity.
- How you spend your non-work time.

TYPES OF SOCIAL MEDIA

LinkedIn
The professional's social network, LinkedIn is the network preferred by most employers. LinkedIn is a large professional network where members connect with each other, participate in Groups, connect, and interact with each other. LinkedIn has over 460 million members (mid-2017) and is widely viewed as the most business-like and professional of the social networks.
- LinkedIn allows members (both workers and employers) to create profiles and "connections" to each other in an online social network which may represent real-world professional relationships.
- Allows you to get in touch with past colleagues and potential clients and expand your professional network.
- Use your profile as your resume
- Find and apply to jobs
- Find and connect with new professionals
- Participate in relevant groups
- Blog about what you know as well as read what others blog about

- On LinkedIn, the basic type of connection is a contact you know personally and who you trust on a professional level. Once you've "connected" to them on LinkedIn, you are considered a 1st-degree connection. You also have an extended network of connections made up of people that your connections know.

Facebook

Facebook is a social networking website and service where users can post comments, share photographs and links to news or other interesting content on the Web, play games, chat live, and even stream live video. Shared content can be made publicly accessible, or it can be shared only among a select group of friends or family, or with a single person.

- Facebook allows you to maintain a friends list and choose privacy settings to tailor who can see content on your profile.
- Facebook allows you to upload photos and maintain photo albums that can be shared with your friends
- Facebook supports interactive online chat and the ability to comment on your friend's profile pages, sometimes called "walls," in order to keep in touch, share information or just to say "hi."
- Facebook supports group pages, fan pages and business pages that let businesses use Facebook as a vehicle for social media marketing.
- Facebook's developer network delivers advanced functionality and monetization options.
- Facebook Connect allows websites to interact with Facebook and allows Facebook to be used as a universal login authentication service.
- You can stream video live using Facebook Live.

Instagram

Instagram is a social media platform for sharing photos, videos, and stories with followers. Users can express creativity, connect with others, and explore global trends through hashtags and Reels. Popular with individuals, influencers, and businesses, Instagram fosters engagement, visual storytelling, and community building through likes, comments, and direct messaging.

Twitter

- Twitter is a free micro-blogging tool that allows users to publish short messages (140 characters or less) through their computers and mobile phones. Twitter launched in 2007, and nearly 1 million people were using it within one year of its debut. Currently, there are more than 313 million people using Twitter.
- People who use Twitter write short messages, called Tweets, which they publish either publicly (for all Twitterers to see) or privately (for only certain Twitterers to see).
- Typically, users will sign up to follow other users whose Tweets they enjoy. For this reason, Twitter can be a great tool for networking, relationship-building, and promoting blogs.
- Businesses also use Twitter to promote products and services and offer real-time customer service.

SOCIAL MEDIA DO'S AND DON'T'S

DO'S
- Use social media to show your knowledge in your field and expand your network.
- Set up a LinkedIn account with a strong summary.
- Join and participate in several groups related to your career interests.
- Get as many LinkedIn references as you can.
- Follow companies in your industry and "like' them.
- Do searches for keywords relevant to what you're looking for.
- Set up a Twitter and/or an Instagram account
- Do searches for those keywords and relevant companies
- Tweets/retweets and posts/reposts links to articles relevant to your followers' interests
- Comment on tweets and ask followers relevant questions

DON'T'S
- Don't forget that everything you put online stays out there somewhere, and anyone – prospective employers, former bosses, etc. – can see it.
- Don't use a physical attribute-flaunting photo better suited to a dating site than a professional networking site.
- Don't refer to yourself in your LinkedIn profile or Twitter headline as "unemployed" or "job seeker."
- Don't throw every noun you can think of to describe yourself in your social media profiles
- Don't forget to check out Google Plus, Pinterest, and other social networking sites as well
- Don't just broadcast "stuff." Be intentional.
- Don't start an account and never update it.

What type(s) of social media do you use? How frequent do you use it/them?

COMMUNICATION

Communication is simply the act of transferring information from one place to another. Communication includes the sharing of information from one person (the speaker) to another person (the listener). Conversation occurs when there is an exchange of information between individuals.

LISTENING

Being a good listener is one of the best ways to be a good communicator. No one likes communicating with someone who only cares about putting in her two cents and does not take the time to listen to the other person. If you're not a good listener, it's going to be hard to comprehend what you're being asked to do.

The Listening Process
- Listening within a work context is the process by which you gain an understanding of the needs, demands, and preferences of your stakeholders through direct interaction.
- Stakeholders might include your boss, clients, customers, co-workers, subordinates, upper management, board members, interviewers, and job candidates.

To be a good active listener in the workplace, there are two components for success: attention and reflection.

- **Attentive listening** includes eye contact, posture, facial expressions, gestures, and genuine interest in what the person is saying.
- **Reflection** includes repeating and paraphrasing what you have heard, showing the person that you truly understand what has been said.

GOOD LISTENING vs BAD LISTENING

Good Listener
- Actively endeavor to understand what others are really trying to say, regardless of how unclear the messages might be.
- interpret nonverbal cues such as tone of voice, facial expressions, and physical posture.
- Allows others to know that they have been heard, and encourages them to share their thoughts and feelings fully.
- Carefully listen to the interviewer's questions in their entirety before responding without interruption.

Bad Listener
- Interrupts the person you're speaking with and talking before they have had a chance to finish what they are saying.
- Responds with a statement that doesn't answer the question.
- Monopolizes the conversation.
- Seeks to be heard and not to understand.

> Are you a good listener or a bad listener? What are some ways you can improve your listening skills?

NONVERBAL COMMUNICATION

Nonverbal communication is the behavior and elements of speech aside from the words themselves that transmit meaning. Non-verbal communication includes:
- Pitch, speed, tone, and volume of voice
- Gestures and facial expressions
- Body posture, stance, and proximity to the listener
- Eye movements and contact
- Dress and appearance

Research suggests that only a 5 percent effect is produced by the spoken word, 45 percent by the tone, inflection, and other elements of voice, and 50 percent by body language, movements, eye contact, etc.

Communicating at Job Interviews

Your nonverbal communication can either support the tone of your conversation or leave the interviewer wondering whether you're all talk and no substance. Displaying nonverbal behaviors that are a match for your messages can help you convince employers that you are genuinely interested in the job and suited for the work. In general, what's most important is to be positive and engaging. If you feel confident about your ability to do the job and know you'll be an asset to the employer, you can show that by your actions as well as your words.

Communicating at Work

In addition to making a hiring decision, employers will also be evaluating your nonverbal skills to determine whether you will be able to relate effectively to clients, co-workers, and business associates. In many occupations, the ability to establish credibility and trust is a significant success factor. Positive nonverbal behavior will enable you to demonstrate your sincerity and engaging personality.

EXAMPLES OF NONVERBAL COMMUNICATION SKILLS

- Avoiding a slouching posture
- Avoiding smiling or laughter when messages are serious
- Displaying some animation with hands and facial expressions to project a dynamic presence
- Don't bring your phone, a drink, or anything else to an interview or meeting that could distract you
- Don't interrupt your interviewer
- Eliminating fidgeting and shaking of limbs
- Establishing frequent but not continuous or piercing eye contact with interviewers
- Focusing on the conversation
- Introducing yourself with a smile and a firm handshake
- Keeping hands away from the face and hair
- Leaning slightly forward to indicate interest
- Listening carefully
- Maintaining open arms, folded arms can convey defensiveness
- Modulating vocal tone to express excitement and punctuate key points
- Nodding to demonstrate understanding
- Observing the reaction of others to your statements
- Paying attention to the conversation
- Reading the nonverbal signals of others; providing clarification if they look confused, wrapping up if they have heard enough
- Refraining from forced laughter in response to humor
- Refraining from looking at the clock, your phone, or displaying any other signs of disinterest
- Respecting the amount of personal space preferred by your communication partners
- Rotating eye contact to various speakers in group interviewing or networking situations
- Shaking hands firmly without excessive force
- Showing that you're interested in what the interviewer is telling you
- Smiling to indicate that you are amused or pleased with a communication
- Staying calm even when you're nervous
- Steering clear of monotone delivery
- Waiting until the person is done talking to respond

List several of your nonverbal communication skills:

Do you see a need to improve your nonverbal communication skills? If so, how do you plan to improve them?

COMMUNICATION TIPS

Clarity and Concision
Good communication means saying just enough - don't say too little or talk too much. Try to convey your message in as few words as possible. Say what you want clearly and directly, whether you're speaking to someone in person, on the phone, or via email. If you ramble on, your listener will either tune you out or will be unsure of exactly what you want. Think about what you want to say before you say it; this will help you to avoid talking excessively and/or confusing your audience.

Friendliness
Through a friendly tone, a personal question, or simply a smile, you will encourage your coworkers to engage in open and honest communication with you. It's important to be nice and polite in all your workplace communications. This is important in both face-to-face and written communication. When you can, personalize your emails to coworkers and/or employees - a quick "I hope you all had a good weekend" at the start of an email can personalize a message and make the recipient feel more appreciated.

Confidence
It is important to be confident in all of your interactions with others. Confidence assures your coworkers that you believe in and will follow through with what you are saying. Exuding confidence can be as simple as making eye contact or using a firm but friendly tone (avoid making statements sound like questions). Of course, be careful not to sound arrogant or aggressive. Be sure you are always listening to and empathizing with the other person.

Empathy
Even when you disagree with an employer, coworker, or employee, it is important for you to understand and respect their point of view. Using phrases as simple as "I understand where you are coming from" demonstrates that you have been listening to the other person and respect their opinions.

Open-Mindedness
A good communicator should enter any conversation with a flexible, open mind. Be open to listening to and understanding the other person's point of view, rather than simply getting your message across. By being willing to enter into a dialogue, even with people with whom you disagree, you will be able to have more honest, productive conversations.

Respect
People will be more open to communicating with you if you convey respect for them and their ideas. Simple actions like using a person's name, making eye contact, and actively listening when a person speaks will make the person feel appreciated. On the phone, avoid distractions and stay focused on the conversation.

Convey respect through email by taking the time to edit your message. If you send a sloppily written, confusing email, the recipient will think you do not respect them enough to think through your communication with them.

Feedback
Being able to appropriately give and receive feedback is an important communication skill. Managers and supervisors should continuously look for ways to provide employees with constructive feedback, be it through email, phone calls, or weekly status updates. Giving feedback involves giving praise as well - something as simple as saying "good job" or "thanks for taking care of that" to an employee can greatly increase motivation.

Picking the Right Medium
An important communication skill is to simply know what form of communication to use. For example, some serious conversations (layoffs, changes in salary, etc.) are almost always best done in person. You should also think about the person with whom you wish to speak - if they are very busy people (such as your boss, perhaps), you might want to convey your message through email. People will appreciate your thoughtful means of communication and will be more likely to respond positively to you.

> **Which medium of communication is your preference? Why?**
>
>
> **Which medium of communication is your least preference? Why?**
>
>
> **How can you improve your overall communication skills?**

ELEVATOR SPEECH / PITCH

- An elevator speech is a clear, brief message or "commercial" about you. It communicates who you are, what you're looking for, and how you can benefit a company or organization. It's typically about 30 seconds; the time it takes people to ride from the top to the bottom of a building in an elevator.

- The idea behind having an elevator speech is that you are prepared to share this information with anyone, at any time, even in an elevator. At a career fair, you can use your speech to introduce yourself to employers.

- It is important to have your speech memorized and practiced. Rehearse your 30-second elevator speech with a friend or in front of a mirror. The important thing is to practice it OUT LOUD. You want it to sound natural. Get comfortable with what you have to say so you can breeze through it when the time comes. This elevator speech is:
    –absolutely no longer than 25 to 30 seconds or - in words - approximately 80 to 90 words •or - in sentences - 8 to 10 brief sentences

WHAT TO SAY

- Your elevator speech should be brief. Restrict the speech to 30 to 60 seconds. that's the time it takes to ride an elevator, hence the name.
- You need to be persuasive. Even though it's a short pitch, your elevator speech should be persuasive enough to spark the listener's interest in your idea, organization, or background.
- Share your skills. Your elevator pitch should explain who you are and what qualifications and skills you have. Try to focus on assets that add value in many situations. This is your chance to brag a bit — avoid sounding boastful, but do share what you bring to the table.

- Practice, practice, practice. The best way to get comfortable with an elevator speech is to practice it until the speed, and "pitch" come naturally, without sounding robotic. You will become comfortable varying the conversation as you practice with it. Try saying your speech to a friend or record it. This will help you know if you are staying within the time limit and giving a coherent message.
- Be flexible. You aren't interviewing for a specific position, so you want to appear open-minded and flexible. It's your chance to make a great first impression with a potential employer.
- Mention your goals. You don't need to get too specific. A overly targeted goal isn't helpful, since your pitch will be used in many circumstances, and with many different types of people. But do remember to say what you're looking for. For instance, you might say, "a role in accounting" or "an opportunity to apply my sales skills to a new market" or "relocate to San Francisco with a job in this same industry."
- Know your audience and speak to them. In some cases, using jargon can be a powerful move — it demonstrates your industry knowledge. But be wary of using jargon during an elevator pitch, particularly if you're speaking to recruiters, who may find the terms unfamiliar and off-putting.
- Have a business card ready. If you have a business card, offer it at the end of the conversation as a way to continue the dialog. A copy of your resume, if you're at a job fair or professional networking event, will also show your enthusiasm and preparedness.

WHAT NOT TO SAY
- Don't speak too fast. Yes, you only have a short time to convey a lot of information. But don't try to fix this dilemma by speaking fast. This will just make it hard for listeners to absorb your message.
- Avoid rambling. This is why it's so important to practice your elevator speech.
- While you don't want to over-rehearse, and sound stilted and robotic, you also don't want to have unfocused or unclear sentences in your pitch or get off-track.
- Don't frown or speak in a monotone. Here's one of the downsides to rehearsing: it can leave you more focused on remembering the exact words you want to use, and less on how you're carrying yourself. Keep your energy level high, positive, and enthusiastic. Modulate your voice to keep listeners interested and keep your facial expression friendly.
- Don't restrict yourself to a single elevator pitch. Maybe you're interested in pursuing two fields — public relations and content strategy. Many of your communication skills will apply to both fields, but you'll want to tailor your pitch depending on who you are speaking to. You may also want to have a more casual, personal pitch prepared for social settings.

ELEVATOR SPEECH SAMPLES

Use these examples as guidelines in crafting your own elevator pitch. Make sure your speech includes details on your background, as well as what you'll provide an employer.

- I recently graduated from college with a degree in communications. I worked on the college newspaper as a reporter, and eventually, as the editor of the arts section. I'm looking for a job that will put my skills as a journalist to work.

- I have a decade's worth of experience in accounting, working primarily with small and midsize firms. If your company is ever in need of an extra set of hands, I'd be thrilled to consult.

- My name is Bob, and after years of working at other dentists' offices, I'm taking the plunge and opening my own office. If you know anyone who's looking for a new dentist, I hope you'll send them my way!

- I create illustrations for websites and brands. My passion is coming up with creative ways to express a message, and drawing illustrations that people share on social media.

- I'm a lawyer with the government, based out of D.C. I grew up in Ohio, though, and I'm looking to relocate closer to my roots, and join a family-friendly firm. I specialize in labor law and worked for ABC firm before joining the government.

- My name is Sarah, and I run a trucking company. It's a family-owned business, and we think the personal touch makes a big difference to our customers. Not only do we guarantee on-time delivery, but it's me and my father answering the phones, and not an automated system.

Write your elevator speech and commit it to memory:

3 Things You Cannot Recover:
*The **WORD** after it is said.*
*The **MOMENT** after it is missed.*
*The **TIME** after it is gone.*

WORK ETHICS & ETIQUETTE

Work ethics include not only how one feels about their job, career, or vocation, but also how one does his/her job or responsibilities. This involves attitude, behavior, respect, communication, and interaction; how one gets along with others. Work ethics demonstrate many things about who and how a person is.

Essentially, work ethics break down to what one does or would do in a particular situation.

Work ethics include but are not limited to:
- honesty (not lying, cheating, and stealing)
- accountability
- doing a job well
- valuing what one does
- having a sense of purpose
- feeling/being a part of a greater vision

Philosophically, if one does not have proper work ethics, a person's conscience may be bothered. People for the most part have good work ethic(s); we should not only want to do, but desire to do the proper thing in a given situation.

ETHICS IN THE WORKPLACE

Workplace ethics and behavior are a crucial part of employment, as both are aspects that can assist a company in its efforts to be profitable. In fact, ethics and behavior are just as important to most companies as performance as high morale and teamwork are two ingredients for success. Every business in every industry has certain guidelines to which its employees must adhere and frequently outline such aspects in employee handbooks.

Behavior
All companies specify what acceptable behavior is, and what is not, when hiring an employee. Many even summarize expected conduct in job descriptions or during the interview process. Behavior guidelines typically address topics, such as harassment, work attire, and language. Workers who don't follow codes of conduct may receive written and verbal warnings and ultimately be fired.

Integrity
A key component of workplace ethics and behavior is integrity, or being honest and doing the right thing at all times. For example, health care employees who work with mentally or physically challenged patients must possess a high degree of integrity, as do those who manage and work primarily with money. Workers with integrity also avoid gossip and sneakiness while on the job.

Accountability
Taking responsibility for your actions is another major factor when it comes to workplace ethics and behavior. That means showing up on scheduled workdays, as well as arriving on time and putting in an honest effort while on the job. Workers who exhibit accountability are honest when things go wrong, then work toward a resolution while remaining professional all the while.

Teamwork
A vital aspect of the workplace is working well with others. That includes everyone from peers to supervisors to customers. While not all employees will always like each other, they do need to set aside their personal or even work-related differences to reach a larger goal. In many instances, those who are not considered "team players" can face demotion or even termination. On the other hand, those who work well with others often can advance on that aspect alone, with teamwork sometimes even outweighing performance.

Commitment
Ethical and behavioral guidelines in the workplace often place a high amount of importance on dedication. Although possessing the necessary skills is essential, a strong work ethic and positive attitude toward the job can carry you a long way. Plus, dedication is often viewed in the business world as "contagious," meaning employees who give a strong effort can often inspire their co-workers to do the same.

Workplace ethics and behavior are a crucial part of employment, as both are aspects that can assist a company in its efforts to be profitable. In fact, ethics and behavior are just as important to most companies as performance as high morale and teamwork are two ingredients for success. Every business in every industry has certain guidelines to which its employees must adhere and frequently outline such aspects in employee handbooks.

A strong work ethic is vital to a company achieving its goals. Every employee, from the CEO to entry-level workers, must have a good work ethic to keep the company functioning at its peak. A work ethic is a set of moral principles that an employee uses in their job. Certain factors come together to create a strong work ethic.

- Behavior
- Integrity
- Accountability
- Teamwork
- Respect

- Commitment
- Responsibility
- Quality
- Discipline

RATE YOUR WORK ETHICS (10 being the highest)	1	2	3	4	5	6	7	8	9	10
Trustworthy										
Respectful										
Honest										
Responsible										
Fair										
Caring										
Accountable										
Value my work										
Have a sense of purpose										
Team player										
Disciplined										
Committed										
Efficiently manage time										
Flexible										
Adaptable										

How can you improve upon either of the work ethics listed above?

CHARACTERISTICS OF EFFECTIVE TEAMWORK

"Coming together is a beginning. Keeping together is progress. Working together is success."
-- Henry Ford

Unified Commitment to a Goal
- A team is created to complete the goals it is given. An effective team is committed to completing its goal by using the team's resources. It does not mean that as individuals the people that make up the team share the same point of view or are all in agreement on what is best for the group. It means that when the team is presented with a goal, they can come together and work as a single unit to complete the task.

Respect
- Team members who have self-respect and respect others can operate with clarity by being honest without the expectation of an emotional response.

Participation
- In order for a team to act as a team, everyone must be participating in the creation of a solution. A team does not have extra members. Each member of a team is essential to the team's success, and when the group is given a task, each member knows what their job is and sets out to put in their fair share of the effort.

Open Communication
- A team is able to communicate effectively and there is a feeling of open communication between all members of the group. Issues within a team are handled by face-to-face communication. Team members do not talk behind each other's backs as there is a respect developed among team members that necessitates direct and open communication on all issues.

Decision-Making
- A team has a hierarchy and a built-in decision-making system that helps it to react quickly and effectively to all situations. The members of the group are respected for their various areas of expertise, and the leader of the group has developed the ability to obtain the group members' opinions to formulate the group's response. This applies to decisions made within the group, ranging from resolving internal conflict to a potential change in group leadership.

Efficient Use of Ideas
- Brainstorming is one way that groups come up with a solution to a problem. An effective team is able to gather information from each member and formulate that information into a response. The team becomes adept at dismissing ideas that will not work and including effective ideas into what would become the team's solution to an issue.

Do you work better alone or as a team? Why or why not?

What positives do you have to bring to a team environment?

TIME MANAGEMENT
- "Time management" is the process of organizing and planning how to divide your time between specific activities. Good time management enables you to work smarter – not harder – so that you get more done in less time, even when time is tight and pressures are high. Failing to manage your time damages your effectiveness and causes stress.

EFFECTS OF PROPER TIME MANAGEMENT
- Greater productivity and efficiency.
- A better professional reputation.
- Less stress.
- Increased opportunities for advancement.
- Greater opportunities to achieve important life and career goals.

EFFECTS OF POOR TIME MANAGEMENT
- Missed deadlines.
- Inefficient workflow.
- Poor work quality.
- A poor professional reputation and a stalled career.
- Higher stress levels.

> What are some things you can do to improve your time management skills?

FLEXIBILITY AND ADAPTABILITY

Adaptability is the nature of **changing or creating modifications** in oneself to suit the new environment. It's a sought-after skill as it indicates the employee can adapt to changing customer needs and technological trends. It is also tied to career growth as the person becomes more equipped. For a workplace culture, it means that a person must be:
- open to new ideas or changes.
- able to work independently or in teams, carry out tasks that are not intended for one person only. Employers are increasingly shifting from single roles to rotation of roles and flexible job descriptions.

Flexibility at workplace allows one to evaluate what is happening and adjust to the role and responsibilities or even the job being offered.

ADAPTABLE
- Fit the Culture
- Make or break deal
- More productive
- Job requirement
- Highly valued
- Better job security

FLEXIBLE
- Open to trend
- Not rigid in thoughts
- Adjusting to situations
- Effective problem solving
- Able to negotiate
- Work under pressure
- Able to communicate
- Acknowledging others' views
- Allow expanding
- Able to learn
- Balancing work with family
- More productive
- Optimistic
- Diversity valued
- Use a different approach
- Accommodate job rotation
- Shows confidence
- Able to transcend

WORKPLACE ETIQUETTE

Workplace etiquette is expected behaviors and expectations for individual actions within society, group, or class. Within a place of business, it involves treating coworkers and employers with respect and courtesy in a way that creates a pleasant work environment for everyone.

- **Respect your coworkers' privacy.** Peering over a coworker's cubicle to grab his or her attention is a no-no. Always act as if your peers were guarded by doors and make a knock-knock motion before you enter his or her desk area. What's more, steer clear of your peers' possessions, too. "Whether it's a text, email, snail mail, or paper on the printer or a desk, if your name isn't on it, don't read it, touch it, or share it."

- **Ask before you borrow anything.** We've all borrowed a peer's pen in a bind—only never to return it. But nothing raises the ire of your coworkers quicker than borrowing—and losing—their property without their permission. So, "remember what your parents taught you as a child. "Never borrow something without asking, and if you do, be sure to return it as soon as possible."

- **Stand up to show respect.** When your boss enters the conference room, don't keep your nose buried in your phone. You should stand to greet him or her. The same idea applies when anyone enters your office. No matter where you are or whom you're greeting, standing is a sign of respect

- **Don't email time-sensitive information.** You need a colleague to send you a copy of a report—stat. But instead of walking the five feet to her cubicle, you shoot her an email. This tends to be a millennial move because they often try to avoid face-to-face encounters with coworkers like the plague. It may seem more practical to send a text [or email], but you risk being seen as lazy and lacking social or communication skills—which is not exactly a way to garner respect.

- **Give thanks.** Handwritten notes of any kind may seem like a lost art, but it's time to resurrect at least one in the office: the handwritten thank-you note. A written thank-you note is a low-cost, high-impact way to show your professionalism. Send one to thank a potential employer for an interview, your coworker for being a peerless partner, or your boss for finally giving you that raise.

- **Keep your voice down.** You could simply be discussing a project passionately. But raising your voice while you're talking—or going hands-free by using the speaker feature on your phone—is a distraction to your peers. You're telling your coworkers that you have zero regard for their work, which is no way to make work friends. If you need to speak loudly, make your way to a conference room or another area of the office.

- **Keep it clean.** Many etiquette faux pas occur in the office kitchen. (Of course, some people commit them in their cubicles, too—for example, your coworker who peels open a stinky pouch of tuna at her desk.) Make a promise to clean up after yourself in shared spaces and avoid bringing smelly foods to work. We think popcorn is OK, though—as long as you share.

What would you do in the following scenarios:
1. Fred knows his employer is going to ask him to do a boring but necessary job.
   Fred should:
      a. Avoid the boss as long as possible by hanging out in the lunchroom, taking a lot of breaks, or hiding in another area of the building.
      b. Clutter up his work area, look frazzled, and loudly complain about how overworked he is.
      c. Sigh, roll his eyes, and accept the job, but then conveniently "forget" to do it.
      d. Accept the task cheerfully and use it as an opportunity to learn more about the job.

2. You are part of a team that has been asked to complete an assignment by a deadline. However, you notice that at least one of your five team members is not doing his/her share of the responsibility. What would you do?

3. A co-worker has been stealing from the company, and after you have caught them in the act on more than one occasion, he has asked you not to tell anyone. What action, if any, would you take? Why?

4. It is 4:45 p.m. and your shift ends at 5:00 p.m. The supervisor asks you to assist with a project that just emerged and needs to be completed before 8:00 p.m. What would your response be?

5. A co-worker was having a bad day, and when you approached him about an assignment, he began using profanity towards you and requested that you leave him alone. Your response?

CURSING IN THE WORKPLACE: 5 Reasons Not to Do It

Consider work a foul-language-free zone. In an office setting, you are surrounded by people of all faiths, backgrounds, and moral codes of conduct. Given this diversity, watch your language by editing out swear words, demeaning phrases, and other offensive remarks. Avoiding curse words will speak volumes about you.

Clean language makes you more promotable. More than half of employers in the CareerBuilder survey said they would be less likely to promote someone who swears on the job. Even if your boss regularly uses curse words at the office, you can't go wrong by keeping a civil tongue.

It demonstrates grace under pressure. If tough situations bring out profanity, find other ways to cope. We all face difficult circumstances at work, but stress-induced swearing will likely lead your coworkers and your boss to seriously question your self-control. Profanity can negatively impact office morale, and directing it at a coworker can put a severe strain on a work relationship.

Others are looking up to you. No matter what your position, you are serving as a role model for others in your office. Habitual swearing is a bad example to set in front of anyone, but especially new hires, interns, and those who are just entering the professional world. While it would be unrealistic to use the word "never" when it comes to using an occasional &%#* word, you don't want to be the one responsible for single-handedly lowering the office's standards.

You are showing respect. You may think your continuous cursing is harmless, but there are most likely people in your office who simply don't want to hear your outbursts. Because this behavior is guaranteed to offend or bother at least a few of your coworkers, use this knowledge as motivation to bite your tongue. Your coworkers may not tell you they are tired of hearing your rants and tirades, but they are certainly forming an opinion of you that is less than desirable.

You appear immature. Teens often use profanity as a way to fit in or to come across as cool to their peers. Sixty-eight percent of employers surveyed believe that employees who swear demonstrate a lack of maturity. It's difficult to be taken seriously as a professional when your coworkers are labelling you as lacking self-discipline every time you spout off because something didn't go your way. Just like your mother taught you, "Use your words and play nice!"

EMAIL ETIQUETTE

Grab the recipient with the subject line. Your word choice in the subject line may determine whether your message gets opened or deleted, so keep it short and to the point. "Thinking of you" or "Hello" will get your email sent to the junk file, as opposed to "Request for follow-up to today's meeting."

Double-check your "TO" line. When email goes awry, it is often because a message was sent to the wrong person with a similar name. We have all heard horror stories of someone hitting "reply all" and sending off private information to a group of people who were not the intended recipients. One additional tip: leave the "TO" field blank until you are ready to send, so you don't accidentally launch the email before you are ready.

Address the person by name. Always double-check spelling (when in doubt, call or do a quick search) before you send. A misspelled name guarantees your email will be deleted immediately. You are trying to establish a personal connection, so using their name is a must. Avoid generic greetings that could be used for anyone, and at all costs, avoid "To Whom It May Concern."

Explain your connection. You might be reaching out to a new contact and want to introduce yourself and your company. Maybe you met them briefly at a networking event and would like to hear more about their business. Perhaps you saw them in the news recently or followed their blog for a few years. If a mutual acquaintance referred you, mention that person by name. In a few words, establish who you are and the shared connection. When appropriate, mention a specific impression the recipient made on you.

Keep it conversational. A warm, friendly tone is critical. Make your email easy to read in simple language instead of trying to dazzle them with technical terms or jargon. Present yourself professionally, with correct spelling, punctuation, and no emoticons.

Keep it short. Even people you already know will wince at the sight of an endless stream of paragraphs. Show the receiver you respect their time enough to keep it concise and to the point.

Be specific. Don't make the recipient wonder what you want. If you are reaching out simply to establish a connection and no call to action is necessary, thank them for their insights on their speech or in their most recent news article. This is a good way to leave the door open for future contact. If you want to take it a step further, be exact: "Can I arrange a 15-minute phone conversation or meet for coffee to discuss some of my ideas?" Asking them for the opportunity to "pick their brain" is vague and self-serving. Don't expect an enthusiastic response.

Use correct grammar, spelling, and punctuation. In business, everything you send out from your office needs to look professional. That means no abbreviations, acronyms, or emoticons. Even if you enjoy a very relaxed relationship with the other person, assume your email may be forwarded; therefore, use a smiley face in careful moderation. Failing to use correct punctuation, spelling, and grammar can have the unintended consequence of making you look either negligent or sloppy. This includes:
- Avoiding the use of all caps unless it's necessary to emphasize a subject or
- section of an email.
- Never use all caps throughout the email, as it can be interpreted as shouting or aggressive.
- Avoiding the use of several exclamation marks (!) at the end of a sentence unless it is sharing some exciting news. Otherwise, it can be seen as aggressive, especially if the sentence is giving a directive.

Be mindful of your tone. Choose your words carefully to avoid anything the reader could perceive as sarcasm or negativity. Be aware that a curt message or response can have the same effect.

Close professionally. End your email with an all-purpose phrase like "Best regards" or "Sincerely." For more informal communication, or when you have an ongoing conversation by email, just sign off with your name. Make sure every email includes a signature line at the end listing your full name and business contact information. Beware of including a quote or a line of scripture below your signature line. These personal sentiments are generally not appropriate in a business setting and can undermine your professionalism.

Follow up. Your email is one among countless others that will land in their inbox on a particular day. If you have included a specific request and don't hear back within a week, follow up with a quick note reminding them of your previous message. With the right approach, emails can get you noticed, generate a response, and lead to a face-to-face meeting. If your offer for coffee or lunch is accepted, be sure to show up with relevant questions - and pick up the check. Express your gratitude for their time.

WORK READINESS PRE-TEST / POST-TEST

1. What is a resume?

   _____
   _____
   _____
   _____

2. What are the 4 types of resumes?

   _____
   _____
   _____
   _____

3. It is professional practice to use symbols, designs, and lots of colors on your resume. T/F

   _____

4. The heading should include
   a. Your email address
   b. Your phone number
   c. Your Social Security number
   d. All of the above

5. The purpose of a cover letter is "not" to
   a. Find out what the job is all about
   b. Provide additional information about your skills and experience
   c. Provide information on why you are qualified for the job
   d. Accompany each resume sent out

6. The cover letter should be formatted like a professional business letter. T/F

7. It is not necessary to send a thank-you letter following an interview. T/F

8. A job interview is a one-on-one interview consisting of a conversation between a job applicant and an _____ which is conducted to assess whether the applicant should be hired.

9. Name 3 types of interviews:

10. Which of the following should you not do during a phone interview?
    a. Smoke, chew gum, eat, or drink
    b. Keep a glass of water handy, in case you need to wet your mouth
    c. Smile
    d. Speak slowly and enunciate clearly

11. Being on time for an interview is an employer's perspective regarding your time management and work ethic. T/F

12. Nonverbal communication includes
    a. Posture
    b. Body language
    c. Eye contact
    d. All of the above
    e. None of the above

13. Preparation plus opportunity equals _____.

14. Networking is a means of marketing yourself. T/F

_____

15. Which of the following are NOT your networks?
    a. Family
    b. Friends
    c. Friend of a friend
    d. None of the above

16. Social media is at the intersection of technology and computers. T/F
_____

17. List three types of social media networks:

_____
_____
_____

18. Communication includes the sharing of information from one person, called the speaker, to another person called the _____.

19. An elevator speech is a clear, brief message or "commercial" about you and communicates who you are, what you're looking for, and how you can benefit a company or organization. T/F

_____

20. Work ethics does not include
    a. honesty (not lying, cheating, and stealing)
    b. accountability
    c. doing a job well
    d. coming to work late

21. Working with others to complete a task is called
    a. Networking
    b. Communicating
    c. Teamwork
    d. Socializing

22. "Time management" is the process of organizing and planning how to divide your time between specific activities. T/F

_____

23. The effects of proper time management include which of the following? (circle all that apply)
    a. Greater productivity and efficiency.
    b. A better professional reputation.
    c. Missed deadlines.
    d. Inefficient workflow.

24. Being flexible and adaptable is not necessary in maintaining employment. T/F

_____

25. Email etiquette includes which of the following? Circle all that apply.
    a. Using correct grammar
    b. Be mindful of your tone
    c. Be specific
    d. Always include an attachment